DUNKIRK
THE REAL STORY IN PHOTOGRAPHS

DUNKIRK

THE REAL STORY IN PHOTOGRAPHS

TIM LYNCH

▣ **mirrorpix**

The History Press

Cover illustrations
Front: Men lining up on the beach awaiting rescue. *Back*:
Evacuated troops aboard a transport ship headed for England.

First published 2017

The History Press
The Mill, Brimscombe Port
Stroud, Gloucestershire, GL5 2QG
www.thehistorypress.co.uk

British Library Cataloguing in Publication Data.
A catalogue record for this book is available from the British
Library.

ISBN 978 0 7509 8273 3

Typesetting and origination by The History Press
Printed in Turkey

CONTENTS

1

PREPARING FOR WAR

On 11 October 1939, just five weeks after the outbreak of war, Leslie Hore-Belisha, the British Minister for War, told Parliament that 'we have fulfilled – and more than fulfilled – our undertaking recently given to France to dispatch to that country in the event of war a British Expeditionary Force of a specified dimension within a specified time'. Britain had, he claimed, transported more men to France than it had in 1914 – supplying 25,000 vehicles of around fifty different types, 'some of them of enormous dimensions and weighing 15 tons apiece or more'. This was not the 'light army' that had gone to France twenty-five years before. 'Nearly sixty per cent of the fighting troops in 1914 were infantrymen,' he said, 'relying on their rifles and bayonets and two machine guns per battalion':

Now only twenty per cent of the fighting troops are infantrymen, with fifty Bren guns and twenty-two anti-tank rifles, and other weapons as well with each battalion. It will be seen from this one example how much more effectively armed with fire-power is the present Expeditionary Force.

It was a masterpiece of the spin-doctor's art.

'Knowing the precise situation regarding the British Field Army in France in general, and in particular in my own division,' wrote Bernard Montgomery, then a major general in command of 3rd Division:

I was amazed to read in a newspaper one day in France in October 1939, the speech of the Secretary of State for War in Parliament when he was announcing the arrival of the BEF [British Expeditionary Force] in France. He gave Parliament and the British people to understand that the Army we had just sent to France was equipped 'in the finest possible manner

which could not be excelled. Our Army is as well if not better equipped than any similar Army.'

It was not a claim likely to impress a man whose troops had been held up at Falmouth by transport officers who refused to accept that regular soldiers of the army's front-line force really needed quite so many laundry vans. Like the rest of the army, 3rd Division was so short of transport that it was going to war in a fleet of lorries and vans commandeered from civilian businesses and hastily repainted green. Montgomery later claimed that his division's progress through France could be mapped by the trail of broken-down transport left stranded along the roadside; indeed, by early 1940, over half the army's transport in France had broken down. As Hore-Belisha was boasting about the vehicles being sent to France, planners had already begun searching for 500 pack animals per division to deliver supplies where motor transport could not go. Since the army had no four-wheel drive vehicles, this meant anywhere not near a road.

It was not just transport. On a visit to the troops of the 42nd (Lancashire) Division, the newly appointed commander of the BEF, Lord Gort, found men eating with their hands because of the lack of cutlery at tables pieced together from corrugated iron. Elsewhere units struggled to obtain boots and uniforms, let alone their full scale of weaponry, and men were forced to use their own money to buy essential items, including binoculars and revolvers. William Harding, a sergeant in the Royal Artillery, recalled how a monotonous diet of bully beef stew eventually forced his officers to start buying food from nearby towns whilst Harding himself led a group of men to forage for anything that could be had from local farms. Even water supplies were inadequate. In some places men took to using the last dregs of their morning tea to shave with. Corps

Best remembered for the 'Belisha Beacon' pedestrian crossing, Secretary of State for War Leslie Hore-Belisha (left) was deeply unpopular with senior figures in the military because of his attempts to reform the army in the 1930s.

A gas-mask fitting for children in Birmingham, October 1939. Among the stores shipped to France by the BEF were stores of poison gas left over from the First World War; the threat of chemical warfare was so great that trials of gas masks for horses, dogs and even cats were under way when war broke out.

British soldiers leaving for France in September 1939.

British soldiers disembark from a troopship in France carrying their kit bags.

Right: Lord Gort (left), commander of the BEF.

Below right: Kingston Council workers repairing a manhole, 1939. Horse-drawn transport was still a common sight on British roads and finding motor transport for the BEF was a serious problem.

Below: Adolf Hitler, leader of the Nazi party and Chancellor of Germany, c. 1939. (Deutsches Bundesarchiv)

Commander Lieutenant General Alan Brooke visited one battalion in November 1939 and reported: 'It would be sheer massacre to commit it to battle in its present state.'

Yet only twenty years earlier, Britain had had the largest, best-equipped and most professional army in its history. Fighting the Great War, though, had left the country almost bankrupt. From August 1919, it was agreed that future defence spending would be based on a policy known as the Ten Year Rule, which assumed 'that the British Empire will not be engaged in any great war during the next ten years, and that no Expeditionary Force is required for that purpose'. In other words, Britain's military would not be needed for at least ten years and could be cut back to the bare minimum. In 1928 Winston Churchill, as Chancellor of the Exchequer, succeeded in making the Ten Year Rule permanent so that now each financial year the clock would automatically be reset back to year one and the armed forces would never get any closer than a decade away from a state of readiness for war. The army's strength in 1919 had stood at 2.5 million men but, by 1932, the budget allowed only 'a number of Land Forces, not exceeding 148,700, all ranks, [will] be maintained for the Service of the United Kingdom at Home and abroad, excluding His Majesty's Indian Possessions (other than Aden), during the year ending on the 31st day of March, 1933'. In other words, the entire army, stationed in garrisons across the empire, was now no larger than the understrength BEF sent to France in the first months of war in 1914.

With all its forces weakened, Britain's home defence planning relied heavily on the French to stop the Germans reaching the Channel. Realising that he could not expect the French to agree to such a policy without something in return, in March 1939 Hore-Belisha openly promised the support of more than nineteen divisions of infantry and tanks that would be sent to France in case of war. The French were delighted by the promise, while the German military attaché was said to have been 'completely stunned'. It was a generous offer but one that was far beyond what the depleted British military could achieve. It would take around eighteen months to prepare a force that size, even if the money to equip and train them was suddenly made available.

New volunteers for the army in Newcastle.

Highlanders prepare to leave for France in September 1939. Many of these men would fight on after the last boats had left Dunkirk.

468   *The War Illustrated*   *December 18th, 1939*

How the British Soldier of 1939 Goes to War

STEEL HELMET
2½ lbs.

ANTI-GAS CAPE
3½ lbs.

RESPIRATOR
(in "ALERT" Position)
3½ lbs.

HAVERSACK
& CONTENTS
5 lbs.

STRAPS, BELT etc.
3½ lbs.

POUCHES
(Each containing
60 Rounds Bren
Gun ammunition)
10 lbs each.

BAYONET
& SCABBARD
1¾ lbs.

RIFLE
8 lbs 10½ ozs.

THE "battle dress" of the British Army was finally approved in April 1939, and is now worn by both men and officers. It is a two-piece garment of khaki serge, consisting of a blouse and trousers buckling at the wrists and ankles, the ankles also being protected by web anklets. The weight of the uniform is about 12 lb. This soldier is wearing battle dress, but is not completely equipped. When wearing full marching order, the infantryman carries a valise (or pack) on his back in place of the haversack seen here, the latter being transferred to the left hip above the bayonet and counter-balanced on the right by a water-bottle. The valise holds the great-coat, cardigan when not worn, and such other personal effects as individual skill in packing can get into it; while in the haversack are a hold-all with comb, tooth-brush, shaving outfit, fitted housewife, socks, mess tin, emergency ration, etc. The large patch pocket on the trousers is to hold maps and papers. Though officers carry some additional articles of equipment, such as revolvers and binoculars and compasses, there is nothing in their uniform to distinguish them from the men except the shoulder badge.

ANKLE BOOTS
4¾ lbs.

Specially photographed for THE WAR ILLUSTRATED under War Office supervision

Above: A British Army unit prepares to move to France. (Author's collection)

Left: Although the BEF were supposed to be issued the modern '1937 pattern' equipment and uniforms, many were still using surplus stores from the First World War. (Author's collection)

THE MAGINOT LINE

Named after the French Minister of War André Maginot, the Maginot Line was a line of seemingly impregnable fortifications along the French side of the border with Germany. It was an enormous network of forts deep underground linked by railway tunnels and roads and supported by ammunition dumps, gun emplacements and even railway-mounted artillery guns in a defence zone up to 16 miles wide. Below ground, troops lived in air-conditioned barracks and were even given sunlamp treatment to cope with their underground lifestyle. The forts of the Maginot Line were heavily protected from any sort of attack and designed so that their garrisons could hold out for weeks or even months.

Across the Channel, British planners watched the building of the Maginot Line with interest. Ideally, it was suggested, Britain should encourage France to extend its Maginot Line defences from Longuyon on the Luxemburg border – where the fortifications currently ended – to the Channel coast. It would not be possible to build heavy forts in the lowland areas along the Franco–Belgian border, but other types of defences were considered possible. Since the size and effectiveness of the French defence line would have a direct impact on the need to prepare and deploy the BEF, the stronger the line, the less Britain would need to contribute. 'It is therefore a strong French interest to cover them by an extension of the Maginot Line [to the coast],' Cabinet Secretary Lord Hankey wrote. 'Incidentally it is a strong British interest, but it would be advisable not to say so or else the French might ask us to pay!'

In what Captain Mainwaring would later call a 'typical shabby Nazi trick', the Germans did not attempt to force their way through the Maginot Line but instead simply drove around the end of it. What was often presented as a joke by the British was, in fact, precisely what the French wanted to happen. The idea was to force any invasion to come through neutral Belgium or Switzerland so that the war could be fought in those countries. France was counting on being able to fight a long war that would drain Germany of its resources, forcing its economy to collapse, after which France would be able to attack and overrun its enemy.

Unfortunately, the Germans had very different ideas about what would happen next.

"This is French for 'You Can't Take It'!

PHONEY WAR

When German troops invaded Poland on 1 September 1939, both Britain and France were quick to mobilise their forces in readiness for the German attack. Across Britain thousands of evacuees left London, expecting bombing to start at any moment. British, French, Belgian, Dutch and German forces made ready and waited for orders. Waited. And waited. Watching the inactivity from across the Atlantic, US Senator William Borah told a newspaper that, in his opinion, 'there is something phoney about this war'.

The phrase quickly caught on. As the skies over England remained stubbornly clear of the dreaded masses of enemy bombers, and embarrassed evacuees returned home, the older generation recalled events in South Africa forty years earlier and began to refer to what was going on across the Channel as 'the bore war'. Seizing on the German propaganda about their 'lightning war' tactics in Poland, the British press wrote about a new style of war – 'Sitzkrieg'. Even the French began to speak about la drôle de guerre or 'the strange war'.

Stories spread that the Germans could not attack because their tanks were made of cardboard and papier mâché for propaganda films, and many admitted that if the Germans did come, they wouldn't have been able to tell them apart from the Belgians, who wore a similar grey uniform. As time went on, despite a few false alarms, the chance of a shooting war seemed to become more and more remote.

For the troops of the BEF, the whole thing took on the air of an extended summer camp rather than service in a war zone. For those able to visit the fleshpots of Lille, vin blanc (or 'plonk' as the men called it) was available at just 1 franc a glass and a bottle of champagne could be had for 3s 6d (less than 40p). The cafés familiar to their fathers and uncles were still providing egg and chips with bread, butter and coffee for 8d (about 4p today). A vigorous campaign was launched warning of the dangers of spending too much time in the many brothels advertising their services, but nevertheless business remained good.

But for all its attractions, France was not home and as the weather worsened the opportunities to visit towns became fewer. More and more time was spent at base, digging trenches or standing guard against the saboteurs rumoured to be infiltrating the Allied lines. To ease the boredom, the Daily Mirror's 'Cassandra Fund' set out to provide dartboards for every unit, and across the country other papers followed suit, ensuring a steady flow of 'comforts' ranging from socks and mittens to tobacco and Christmas presents.

Throughout one of the worst winters in memory the two sides stared at each other across the German border and wondered what all the fuss was about.

'Strewth, Bill!... What Wouldn't I Give for a Game of Darts

When war finally came, the army that Britain sent to support its French ally was tiny and ill prepared. Despite Hore-Belisha's optimistic offer, by May 1940 he had provided just ten divisions to France – a force equivalent to the Dutch Army but only half that mobilised by neutral Belgium. France, by contrast, had mobilised 117 divisions. Not only were the British troops ill prepared, there was also the problem of what to do with them.

As the junior partner, the BEF came under the control of the French High Command and so were simply added to their plan. In the case of the expected invasion of Belgium, this was to set up a series of defence lines along the banks of the Rivers Dyle and Escaut in an attempt to halt the Germans – in what would be a virtual rerun of the First World War – in the belief that Germany, with few natural resources, would not be able to sustain a long war. The Allies would blockade Germany and use the stalemate to build up their own forces and launch a counterattack, probably in 1941 or '42.

Since Belgium was neutral the Allies could not enter the country to prepare defences or even carry out any reconnaissance of the areas in which they would be expected to fight and so, instead, began work on what would become known as the Gort Line – a series of concrete bunkers along the Franco–Belgian border, named after the commander of the BEF, Lord Gort. If all else failed, the Allies would fall back and hold the Germans there.

Unfortunately, the Germans hadn't agreed to the plan.

Newly called-up recruits report for duty. (Author's collection)

2

THE TRAP IS SET

After nine months of war, the defeat of Anglo-French forces in Norway and a series of false alarms, the BEF was still taken by surprise when, in the early hours of 10 May, German troops crossed the Belgian frontier and began their attack. Captain Gilbert White of the East Surrey Regiment was still in bed when 'suddenly there was a great air raid':

I looked out of the window; searchlights were flicking across the sky, there was a hell of a commotion. I got dressed quickly, went across to battalion HQ immediately and there was great consternation. Signals were coming in and we couldn't get a clear picture in any way, but most of us realised that the Phoney War was over and that the Germans had begun some sort of military operation.

In fact, just after 5 a.m. specially trained German airborne forces had landed gliders on the roof of the Belgian border fortress of Eben-Emael and alongside several vital bridges on the Albert Canal, capturing them and opening the way for tanks and infantry to pour into Belgium.

Below: Soldiers arriving in France, September 1939. (Author's collection)

Below right: Armistice Day 1939. The young men of the BEF would soon be called upon to fight over the same battlefields as their fathers had.

Above left: For thousands of British troops, Christmas 1939 would be spent in camps far from home wondering what the New Year would bring.

Above: Lieutenant General Sir John Dill inspecting soldiers at work digging 'Gort Line' trenches during the winter of 1939–40.

Left: Men of the Sherwood Foresters line up for dinner. With only so much that can be done with bully beef, trips to local cafés were eagerly anticipated.

GOVERNMENT IN CRISIS

The German attack came at the worst possible moment for the British. On 8 May, the failure of the government to support the army in Norway led to demands for Prime Minister Neville Chamberlain, and others associated with his pre-war appeasement policy towards Hitler's government, to resign. Chamberlain arrogantly accepted the challenge and called 'on my friends to support me in the lobby tonight'. Reducing a serious debate to a popularity contest, Chamberlain's hubris destroyed any chance he had of retaining his position.

With a good standing amongst members of all parties, Churchill, who himself shared much of the blame for what had gone wrong, spoke loyally in support of Chamberlain but had already been advised that he 'should not be too convincing'. That night, despite the open resentment of the Conservative chief whip, almost every Tory MP in uniform – and at least one in tears – filed into the opposition lobby to vote against their own government. Ten minutes after the division bell rang, the votes had been counted: 281 against the government, 200 for.

After two days of confusion, during which time German troops began their invasion of Belgium, Churchill met with the King at Buckingham Palace to accept the post of prime minister.

"Don't Shoot the Pianist – He's Doing His Best!"

'BLOOD, TOIL, TEARS AND SWEAT'

We are in the preliminary stage of one of the greatest battles in history ... That we are in action at many points – in Norway and in Holland – that we have to be prepared in the Mediterranean. That the air battle is continuous, and that many preparations have to be made here at home.

I would say to the House as I said to those who have joined this government: I have nothing to offer but blood, toil, tears and sweat. We have before us an ordeal of the most grievous kind. We have before us many, many long months of struggle and of suffering.

You ask, what is our policy? I will say: It is to wage war, by sea, land and air, with all our might and with all the strength that God can give us; to wage war against a monstrous tyranny, never surpassed in the dark and lamentable catalogue of human crime. That is our policy. You ask, what is our aim? I can answer in one word: Victory. Victory at all costs – Victory in spite of all terror – Victory, however long and hard the road may be, for without victory there is no survival.

Winston Churchill, 13 May 1940

Above right: Plans to hold the Germans in Belgium were expected to be a replay of the First World War. Here men of the Royal Scots prepare their trenches.

Right: German troops disembarking in Oslo during the invasion of Norway, 9 April 1940.

A Warning Order to French forces to prepare to move had been issued at 5.45 a.m., three hours after bombing raids on Dutch and Belgian targets had begun and twenty minutes after the first gliders landed on Eben-Emael. It then took another thirty minutes for French commander General Gamelin to give the order to put Plan D – the advance to planned positions along the River Dyle – into operation. British headquarters responded by sending a message to all units:

Plan D.J.1. today. Zero hours 1300 hours. 12L. may cross before zero. Wireless silence cancelled after crossing frontier. Command Post opens 1300 hours. Air recces may commence forthwith.

In plain English, it meant Plan D would come into operation at 1 p.m. The 12th Lancers, tasked with leading the move to the River

Above: British soldiers at a concert party during the Phoney War. The French called it 'the joke war' but soon there would be nothing funny about it.

Left: Men of the Border Regiment cleaning a Boys anti-tank rifle (left) and a Bren machine gun, February 1940. The Boys proved to have little effect on German tanks – especially when half-power training ammunition was issued to front-line troops.

Dyle, had permission to start to move before then and units could begin using radios to pass messages once across the frontier. The commander-in-chief, Lord Gort, would set up an advanced command post at the village of Wahagnies and would begin work at 1 p.m. Air reconnaissance flights over Belgium, previously illegal, could begin immediately.

Captain David Strangeways of the Duke of Wellington's Regiment was about to deal with the signaller who had dared to wake him by shouting his name loudly. It took a second or two for him to realise the man wasn't being over familiar; 'David' was the code name of the operation to move forward. After months of preparing for this moment, the BEF responded with an air of excitement, but also with some trepidation, as its men got ready for war. The news spread quickly, but not always in the way that might be expected. Brigadier Archibald Beauman, in charge of the supply lines in northern France, was woken with a cup of tea and the news that the BBC had just reported the war had started.

The men of the 12th Lancers, tasked with spearheading the advance into Belgium and fortified by champagne drunk whilst waiting, roared across the border with their bugler sounding the charge. Behind them came the rest of the BEF, with varying degrees of success. One of Montgomery's 3rd Division units found the frontier barrier closed against them by a border guard who demanded to see their permit to enter Belgium. After a heated debate, in which the guard was assured that the British were not invading his country but coming to its aid because the Germans already had invaded, a British lorry crashed through the barrier and the division roared off to war.

Plan D called for three BEF divisions to form a line along the River Dyle, with five more spaced between the Dyle and the River

Above right: Gordon Highlanders maintaining 'Bren carriers', March 1940. The small, fast armoured vehicles were designed to move Bren machine-gun teams around the battlefield but were no match for Panzer forces.

Right: The carefully prepared defence lines along the Franco-Belgian border were abandoned as the BEF moved forward into Belgium to meet the German invasion. Months of hard work had been wasted. (Author's collection)

Escaut to provide what the military refer to as 'defence in depth'. For the Anglo-French plan to be effective, speed was essential and all emphasis was on getting the men into position as quickly as possible, even at the risk of travelling along public roads in daylight where they would be easy targets for German air attack. Captain Sir Basil Bartlett, serving as a field security officer, was on the Belgian border watching British troops move forward: 'They were travelling at a good speed, but were too closely spaced, I thought. They'd suffer heavily if the Germans took it into their heads to bomb them. There are so far no reports of sabotage on the route.' A few days later, on the 14th, Bartlett's diary noted, 'the weather remains brilliantly fine. The Germans are allowing the BEF to move into its battle positions almost without interference.' Elsewhere, a staff officer of the British air forces in France wrote on 13 May that a 'strange, and I feel, very suspicious feature, has been the extraordinary lack of any German bombing of the BEF and the French armies in their advance through Belgium during the last four days. It looks almost as if the Germans want us where we are going.'

For the troops moving forward, the experience was a mixed one. Belgians lined the streets to welcome the Allies and Arthur Taylor, an RAF man attached to a Royal Artillery unit, recalled being handed drinks and food by cheering crowds and arriving at his destination in a truck festooned with flowers. Captain James Hill of the Royal Fusiliers also remembered being mobbed by Belgian civilians, but 'I found they were pinching what they could off the car'. For the 2nd Battalion of the Durham Light Infantry, the position they were due to occupy seemed ominous as they began to dig trenches around a village called La Tombe. The whole operation had an air of unreality about it. Captain Peter Barclay of the Norfolk Regiment told the lady owner of a chateau that his men needed to dig trenches in her grounds, to which she replied, 'as long as you don't upset the rosebushes and interfere with the rhododendrons I suppose I can't stop you.'

Plans for the defence of the Dyle Line were based on the belief that the fortifications on the Albert Canal and River Meuse would hold the Germans for up to a week, but they had been breached in less than a day and British troops arrived to find Belgian soldiers straggling back among the refugee columns. Then, almost as soon as the Allies were in place, the second phase of the German plan began as another invasion tore through the Ardennes, a region dismissed

FALL GELB (CASE YELLOW)

The German plan for the conquest of the west (*Fall Gelb*) called for an attack by Army Group B into the Netherlands and Belgium in what appeared at first to be exactly the same plan they had used in 1914. Copies of it had fallen into Allied hands a few months earlier when a German plane had crashed and the Allied troop movements to counter what was then seen as an imminent threat were carried out in full view of German reconnaissance planes, confirming what they already suspected the Anglo-French forces would do.

Historians have described the attack as 'the matador's cloak'. Army Group B was intended to draw the bulk of the Allied armies away from their prepared positions and into Belgium. Once the Allied move was complete, Army Group A would make its move. With forty-five of the best-equipped divisions in the German Army, including seven Panzer divisions, its commander, von Runstedt, could call on almost 2,000 tanks to put into action what Erich von Manstein described as a 'revolving door'. As the Allies left their positions heading north and east, the true German attack would push south and west through the Ardennes and across the River Meuse to thrust across France, sever the Allied supply lines and destroy the Allies in a pocket along the coast.

The Allies noticed that their move into Belgium was unopposed by the Luftwaffe but, with all eyes on reaching the Dyle Line, no one noticed the trap that was being set for them.

Right: 'Room for More!' This cartoon appeared in the *Daily Mirror* on 11 May 1940, the day after the start of Operation *Fall Gelb* – the German invasion of the Low Countries.

Below: Lord Gort VC, commander of the BEF. (Author's collection)

Room for More!

by the Allies as unsuitable for tanks and armoured vehicles but now the scene of a massed breakthrough by German Panzer forces supported by hundreds of aircraft. Then all hell broke loose.

The Germans smashed through French lines on the River Meuse and were now in a position to threaten the Allies' right flank. To the north, at Gennep, Dutch policemen escorting a column of German prisoners of war across the bridge on the River Maas turned out to be Special Forces soldiers, and the 'prisoners' were all still fully armed under their greatcoats. The vital bridge was captured in minutes. Heavy bombing raids hit Dutch cities, and paratroopers landed to seize other bridges and airfields. By 14 May, Holland was overrun and surrendered, leaving the left flank of the Allies wide open.

The next day, 25-year-old 2nd Lieutenant Richard 'Dickie' Annand of the Durham Light Infantry was tasked with holding the remnants of a demolished bridge on the River Dyle against a heavy German attack. When the ammunition ran out, his platoon sergeant reported, 'Mr Annand came to me at platoon headquarters and asked for a box of grenades as they could hear Jerry trying to repair the bridge. Off he went and he sure must have given them a lovely time because it wasn't a great while before he was back for more.' He raced forward again and stopped a second attempt, despite having himself been wounded. As the *London Gazette* explained: 'When the order to withdraw was received, he withdrew his platoon, but learning on the way back that his batman was wounded and had been left behind, he returned at once to the former position and brought him back in a wheelbarrow, before losing consciousness as the result of wounds.' Dickie survived his wounds and became the first man to be awarded the Victoria Cross during the Second World War.

However brave the men might be, their position was becoming ever more dangerous. On 16 May Lord Gort received instructions from General Billotte that the British, French and Belgian armies should break off contact with the enemy and over the next couple of nights withdraw to the second planned defence line along the River Escaut.

Ordinary British soldiers could hardly believe that less than a week after their 60-mile advance into Belgium they were now being ordered to withdraw; to them it seemed as if everything was going to plan. News that the Germans had broken through to the south and that to the north Holland had surrendered came as a shock, but there was no sense of panic, just a standard army manoeuvre to adjust the lines. Leaving behind a few men to act as a rearguard, firing a few shots now and again to convince the enemy that the battalions were still in position, the BEF calmly began to fall back.

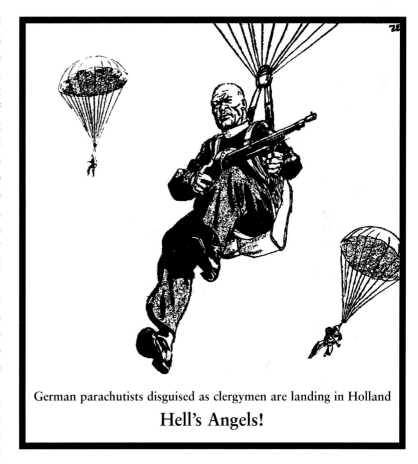

German parachutists disguised as clergymen are landing in Holland

Hell's Angels!

'Hell's Angels!' *Daily Mirror* cartoon, 14 May 1940.

3

'BRIEF AND SUICIDAL'

A year earlier, Britain had promised France an army they did not have, so to make up the numbers 'veterans' battalions' consisting of ageing and unfit reservists were sent to release men from guard duties at headquarters and stores depots. The 9th (Overseas Defence) Battalion of the West Yorkshire Regiment was one such unit sent to the BEF's headquarters at Arras and its battalion commander, Lieutenant Colonel Luxmoore-Ball, was now on his third war. Among his men was Private Gordon Smith who, at the age of 34, had been considered old by infantry standards when he won the Distinguished Conduct Medal back in 1918. Now, at the age of 55, Private Smith would again be called upon to fight in a country he had first seen a generation before. Widely scattered at designated Vulnerable Points around supply dumps and airfields across France, veterans' battalions like the West Yorkshires and the 12th Royal Warwicks were at least made up of trained and experienced soldiers, albeit frequently unarmed and carrying only sticks as deterrents to intruders.

Jim Laidler, an 18-year-old former clerk from Durham who had enlisted in March, arrived in France the following month without even a chance to complete his training when his unit, the Tyneside Scottish, were sent to help build an airfield near the Belgian border. They were part of 23rd Division, one of three partially trained Territorial infantry divisions sent out to act as a labour force on the supply lines but, because they were technically infantry divisions, the British government could also claim to be building up the promised nineteen divisions. Few of the men of 12th, 23rd or 46th Divisions had completed their military training, with some not even having been taught how to use their rifles and most never having fired the Bren machine gun they were equipped with. The agreement had been clear: they were not combat troops and should not be used in battle. But with the trained troops already committed to action on the Dyle Line, as the Panzers swept west there was no one else available to stop them. As the men of 46th Division rushed forward by train from their work on railways and docks in Britanny, 12th Division took up positions around Abbeville at the mouth of the Somme, and 23rd Division set out to defend the Canal du Nord just south of Arras. On 20 May, these men, 'untrained and virtually unarmed' according to one of their own officers, took on the might of the German Panzers.

On the Canal du Nord it quickly became obvious that the position could not be held. The Tyneside Scottish averaged just one Bren gun per platoon and one anti-tank rifle per company, with one 3in mortar between them. They were provided with artillery support, but there were no anti-tank guns at all. Military doctrine held that a fully armed and supported division could be expected to defend no more than about 4 miles of front – 23rd Division was being asked to cover 17 miles. The 'canal' turned out to be an empty ditch, which, according to reports, a car could cross with ease, and a decision was made to withdraw the forward battalions to a better location.

At 7 a.m. on 20 May, the first trucks full of men of the Tyneside Scottish began to withdraw towards Neuville-Vitasse. The terrain was largely open with few defensive features, so that when, at about 8.30 a.m., a force of around twenty tanks of the 8th Panzer Division caught them in a pincer movement, there was little anyone could do. Crowded into lorries and without anti-tank weapons, the Tynesiders and their Durham Light Infantry colleagues took on the tanks with whatever was to hand – Sergeant Chambers was last seen trying to prise open the hatch of a tank with his bayonet to get at the crew inside. It was a one-sided and vicious fight, and the outcome was inevitable. Jim Laidler was with Recruit Company: 'Their ammunition

Above left: German paratroopers dropping into action in Holland. The airborne operation overran Dutch defences in a matter of days, exposing the Allied armies in Belgium to a serious threat to their flank.

Above: An English soldier helping refugees through a burning town in Belgium, following German air raids. The raids created a wave of refugees that hampered efforts to move troops and equipment to the front lines.

Left: British troops in Louvain, Belgium, take advantage of furniture left by refugees to rest in one of the bomb-shattered streets of the town.

Left: A British artillery unit enters Belgium shortly after the German invasion began. (Author's collection)

Below left: German troops using inflatable boats and even rafts improvised from the doors of nearby houses crossed the River Meuse on the first day of the attack. (Author's collection)

expended, a section of recruits with under eight weeks' training calmly obeyed the order to fix bayonets and meet the attack of an enemy [tank] that was approaching them – a futile but heroic gesture. Surrender never occurred to them.' Only around 130 of the 750 Tynesiders eventually made it back to Britain and their sister battalion, the 11th Durham Light Infantry, was equally decimated. When the brigade mustered at the planned rendezvous later that morning just 233 officers and men could be accounted for. There should have been around 2,000.

To the south of the Tynesiders, their colleagues of the West Kents and the Buffs tried to hold their line with just one anti-tank weapon for every 2 miles of front. With no radios available, any semblance of command quickly broke down and each section and platoon began to fight its own battle. It was later shown that isolated pockets of the Buffs had held out for up to two hours and that the anti-tank rifles had stopped at least two tanks before being overrun. At brigade headquarters in the village of Lucheux, Brigadier Roupell, a VC winner from the First World War, sat in the chateau listening to the battle drawing closer. A breathless officer ran in to report tanks approaching but Roupell, trying to maintain control, calmly replied, 'never mind the Germans. I'm going to finish my cup of tea.' At about 6.30 a.m. the sentry on the gate opened fire on a German column and managed to stall it whilst Roupell and his staff escaped through the back door and through the surrounding woods. By then he knew his brigade was lost. Seventy-five men of the 6th Royal West Kents escaped to Britain; 503 were listed as missing; eighty of the 605 Buffs returned.

Another battalion, the 7th Royal West Kents, had been given trucks and made into a mobile force with orders to hold the town of Albert. Joined by the crews of four field guns from a gunnery school, the

A German bomber attacking a road in Belgium. (Author's collection)

column arrived in the main square of Albert at about 6 a.m. to find German tanks in the side streets all around them. The half-charge training rounds they had been given for the anti-tank rifles bounced harmlessly off the Panzers as they closed in for the kill. After the battle, the Germans reported having ambushed a training exercise – after all, the field guns were only supplied with blank ammunition.

Meanwhile, the men of the Royal Sussex Regiment were stuck in a railway siding near Amiens. They had been given orders over a very bad phone connection that they should 'Proceed to Lens'. After a long and difficult journey, during which their train had been bombed and the commanding officer wounded, they arrived to find no one seemed to know what to do with them. After a few frantic calls, their real orders were discovered: 'Proceed Doullens'. They set out again only to discover their train had been shunted into a siding and they were now stuck. By noon on 20 May, German reconnaissance planes had spotted their positions. Soon after, artillery and air strikes began, then the tanks came. They held out until about 8 p.m. in a battle the regimental history called 'brief and suicidal'. When they were finally overrun, one of the battalion's officers refused to raise his hands and was shot as a result. A German officer, impressed by the defiant defence, offered Lieutenant Jackson, who had been wounded four times, a lift in his own car. Despite his pain, Jackson refused to leave his men.

Further west, units of the Queen's Regiment were ordered to defend Abbeville on the mouth of the Somme. The battalions had just three Bren guns and only seven rounds of ammunition for each of their five obsolete anti-tank rifles. As streams of refugees poured out of the town, it was clear that there was little the men could hope to achieve and the decision was taken not to leave them isolated and unsupported but to withdraw south across the Somme. By now, though, Panzers had already appeared.

With their anti-tank rounds soon gone, the men could do nothing as German tanks sprayed their positions with machine-gun fire. Of one battalion of 1,000 men, the commanding officer managed to take about 100 across the debris of a blown bridge. One platoon attempted to escape in trucks but ran into a Panzer group and was mown down. Others swam the river and set up a rope of rifle slings to help others across, but many drowned in the attempt. It would be another three days before the last stragglers reached Rouen. In just one day a brigade of 2,400 men had been reduced to 1,234.

Above: Recruit Company, 1st Battalion Tyneside Scottish. Sent out to France before finishing their training, within weeks these young men armed only with rifles and bayonets would be facing German tanks. (Author's collection)

Opposite:
Top left: German troops leading the attack. (Author's collection)

Bottom left: A German tank during the blitzkrieg advance across France on 20 May. (Author's collection)

Right: Fighting in the French town of Albert. (Author's collection)

The British 'Matilda' tank proved very effective against German Panzers but there were too few of them and not enough radios to help them work as a team with their artillery and infantry support once the Arras attack got under way. (Author's collection)

With a crew of three and armed only with machine guns, the Vickers Light Tank was useful for reconnaissance but could not take on German Panzers armed with far more powerful guns. (Author's collection)

As the Germans broke through at Abbeville, the last of the ill-prepared troops of 46th Division arrived. Travelling in a convoy of trains from their bases in Brittany, 137 Brigade were unaware of what was going on. Former Co-op clerk, 20-year-old Rex Flowers, was among them:

Many trains were passing us on the far line, going in the opposite direction, with all sorts of things besides carriages. Some were filled with French troops, I noticed that they were not in cattle trucks [like us]. Some trains had flat cars with machine guns and artillery on them, mounted and ready for action. But they were going away from the enemy. I wonder if they knew? Some trains were packed with what could only be refugees, hundreds of them. It was incredible! We were getting a bit uneasy, but the penny had not dropped with us yet as to the reason for all this activity!

A raid was taking place on Abbeville and German tanks were already on the outskirts of the town as the first part of the rail convoy passed through; after their train stopped on the outskirts of town, Flowers and his mates realised that the train driver and fireman had run away. The only maps available were those copied onto the backs of cigarette packets from posters in the train carriage and a single copy of *Bradshaw's Railway Guide* carried by one of the men. With only a vague idea of where they were or how to get to their planned destination, the battalion gathered in a railway siding. As they did, a stream of refugees reached them, including a young woman crying hysterically as she forced her way through their ranks. Since the Germans were already ahead of them, the remnants of 137 Brigade joined the refugees and began trudging back along the railway lines, heading to the last town where they had seen British troops. Alongside the track, birds sang as the sun shone on a beautiful spring day. Behind them Abbeville lay in ruins and thousands of British troops lay dead.

By evening, German tank crews had advanced 60 miles in a single day and were posing for photographs on the beaches of the English Channel. The BEF was now cut off from its supply lines – they were doomed.

4

'FRANKFORCE'

On the morning of 21 May, the Germans were in a position to choose between turning south towards the harbours of Dieppe and Le Havre, where the BEF had its main bases, or heading north to capture the vital ports of Boulogne, Calais and Dunkirk and by doing so completely encircle the Allied armies in Belgium. Either way, the Allied armies were now trapped and it would only be a matter of time before they ran out of food, ammunition and fuel. Realising the seriousness of the situation General 'Tiny' Ironside, the Chief of the Imperial General Staff and Britain's most senior soldier, flew to Belgium to meet with Lord Gort and then with French commander-in-chief General Billotte and First Army commander General Blanchard. He later wrote: 'I found Billotte and Blanchard all in a state of complete depression. No plan, no thought of a plan. Ready to be slaughtered. Defeated at the head without casualties ... I lost my temper and shook Billotte by the button of his tunic. The man is completely beaten.' The next day, Billotte left a meeting at Ypres and was involved in a traffic accident, dying after two days in a coma. Hearing the news one senior British officer noted, 'With all respect, he's no loss to us in this emergency.'

Gort was in a difficult situation. It was too late to try to move his divisions south, and in any case that would leave gaps in the line that the Germans would break through. The only realistic option was to

General Georges Blanchard, commander of the French First Army in Belgium and northern France. (Author's collection)

Reinforcements for the BEF embarking on a troop transport ship to bolster the defences on the Franco–Belgium border, *c.* May 1940.

try to launch a counterattack to link up with French forces from the south and try to reconnect with his supply lines south of the River Somme. Taking control at the French headquarters, Ironside ordered General Franklyn to lead 'Frankforce' – an improvised formation of elements of 50th Infantry Division and the 1st Army Tank Brigade – into the attack near Arras. It was a hasty plan. The men of the Durham Light Infantry sent to support the armoured advance had never worked with tanks before and there were few radios available to co-ordinate the infantry, artillery and tank units.

Frankforce set out not knowing that their allies had failed to co-ordinate an attack from the south, although survivors from French 2nd and 3rd Light Armoured Divisions, despite being able to muster just thirty-five tanks between them after days of combat, were eager to fight on and had already signalled their willingness to help. Instead, the attack would go ahead with only the depleted British force taking part. Dividing into two columns, Frankforce set off. Unfortunately, the Phoney War had left its mark and peacetime habits remained. One column of tanks was delayed because a set of railway barrier gates had been left in the closed position and no one was sure what they should do about it.

Despite the delay, the tanks made good progress, leaving the infantry struggling to keep up. Second Lieutenant Peter Vaux commanded the 4th Royal Tank Regiment's Reconnaissance Troop and was thrilled when his tanks caught up with a column of German transport:

They were just as surprised as we were and we were right in amongst them before they knew what was going on. For a quarter of an hour or so there was a glorious free-for-all in which we knocked out quite a lot of their lorries: there were Germans running all over the place. For the most part they were too scared to do very much but some of them had a go at jumping on our tanks and I remember that a German who climbed on the outside of mine was very kindly removed by another tank which turned its machine gun on me and removed him.

The success left Vaux and his men feeling that they could continue all the way to Berlin, and for a time it seemed as if they would. General Erwin Rommel, later to gain fame as the 'Desert Fox', was commanding 7th Panzer Division; he watched his infantry running away and saw artillery guns abandoned when their crews fled and quickly tried to regain some control over his frightened men. So fast was the British advance that Rommel's aide was killed alongside him and Rommel himself was cornered in a shell hole by a British tank – surviving only because the tank driver was mortally wounded and the vehicle ground to a halt. All around, other British units attacked with equal ferocity and success, but there was no way that the battle could be maintained. Without co-ordinated artillery support the infantry did what it could – the Durhams alone took over 400 prisoners during the fighting – but soon the captors found themselves at risk of capture as their momentum wound down and the Germans recovered. The counterattack had failed.

Knowing that defeat was increasingly likely, Ironside began making plans to evacuate guns, ammunition and men from the rear-base depots south of the Somme to ensure that if the worst happened, there would at least be something available with which to defend the British coast from the invasion that would surely follow the fall of France. Ordered out of retirement and instructed to 'get out all you can without alarming the French', General Karslake sailed the next day with a list of priority equipment to save. Convinced that British cities faced being wiped out by massed German bombing, top of that list were anti-aircraft guns to defend against the might of the Luftwaffe. Even before the fighting had begun British planners had considered locating Belgian armouries with a view to stealing away as many of their anti-aircraft guns as they could before the country fell.

Under heavy pressure, the decision was taken to abandon the Escaut Line and to begin to fall back to the prepared bunkers and trenches of the Gort Line. The retreat had begun.

5

BEATING THE RETREAT

By now the situation was worsening by the hour. A new defence line had been established along the La Bassée Canal on the BEF's right flank but it was held by whatever forces happened to be nearby. Around the town of St-Pol, 'Polforce' included men who had been in transit camps on their way to or from leave at home and the men of a mobile bath unit. Around Dieppe, the former patients of an army venereal disease hospital began digging trenches. Untrained Territorials were assigned vital positions in an effort to buy every minute they could to allow the BEF time to move back across Belgium.

Accompanying the BEF was Captain Bredin of the Ulster Rifles, who encountered an unusual problem as his men retreated: Belgian civilians offering them glasses of beer. But although the withdrawal was generally calm, there were constant reminders of how close the enemy were. Crouching in a cornfield, Bredin looked up to see corn stalks sent flying as enemy bullets scythed through just above his head. Elsewhere, though, things were becoming chaotic.

Orders had gone out to evacuate 'useless mouths' – non-essential men who had no combat role and who would just take up rations if they stayed – and naval ships arrived at Boulogne and Calais to begin the process. On 22 May, troops of the Irish and Welsh Guards were brought across from Dover to join the French forces defending the town. They arrived in pouring rain to find the harbour crammed with panic-stricken refugees and stray soldiers, all waiting to rush the ships in their efforts to escape so that the guardsmen had to fix bayonets to force the crowds to part so they could disembark. Taking up positions around the town they were joined by the only other troops available – untrained Pioneers of 5 Group of the Auxiliary Military Pioneer Corps who had originally been ordered there to work as dockers.

The German advance had begun earlier that day and was met by fierce resistance from French troops and RAF fighters, but made steady progress until they gained the high ground overlooking the town from which German artillery could rain shells down into the harbour itself. The situation was hopeless and the next morning, HMS *Keith* and HMS *Vimy* arrived to evacuate the same troops they had delivered the previous day. By then German bombers were overhead and the enemy was so close that naval gunners were firing at the tanks closing in and the ships were under fire from German infantry. Aboard *Vimy*, Able Seaman Don Harris was on the bridge as they followed *Keith* into the narrow harbour:

I noticed our Captain, Lieutenant Commander Donald, train his binoculars on a hotel diagonally opposite but quite close to our ship. I heard another burst of firing from the snipers located in the hotel and then saw our captain struck down. He fell onto his back and as I leapt to his aid I saw a bullet had inflicted a frightful wound to the forehead, nose and eyes of his face. He was choking in his own blood so I moved him onto his side, and it was then I received his final order. It was 'Get the First Lieutenant onto the bridge urgently.' As I rose to my feet more shots from the hotel swept the bridge and the Sub Lieutenant fell directly in front of me. I glanced down and saw four bullet holes in line across his chest. He must have been dead before he hit the deck.

In response, one of *Vimy*'s 4in naval guns blasted the hotel at a range of less than 100yd but the bridge crew were forced to remain lying down on the floor as the ship reversed out of the harbour.

AMPC

To try to meet the demand for men able to act as labourers on the British supply lines in France, a new Auxiliary Military Pioneer Corps (AMPC) was created on 17 October 1939 around a nucleus of reservists considered too old or unfit for front-line service. The corps soon became home to a varied mix of volunteers of German, Austrian or Italian descent (barred from other forms of service), newly called-up conscripts and men who had been recruited straight from similar civilian jobs. They were given little or no military training and issued just one set of uniform for both work and parade, so they quickly gained a reputation for scruffiness and poor discipline. To add insult to injury, three-quarters of the rifles issued to the AMPC were withdrawn due to the shortage of weapons available to newly forming infantry units. By the end of 1939, more than 18,000 AMPC men were working in France, mostly far behind the lines to unload ships, move supplies and build railways and camps for the 'real' soldiers.

The weekly magazine *War Illustrated* explains the role of the newly formed Auxiliary Military Pioneer Corps. (Author's collection)

To add to the terror artillery, heavy bombers and Ju 87 'Stuka' dive-bombers all joined in the attack on the ships of the Dover flotilla, as one by one they made the dangerous trip into the port to pick up as many as they could. Hit amidships and on fire, HMS *Venetia* backed out of the harbour at full speed to avoid blocking the approach, thereby saving hundreds of the men lining the quays. But heroism alone was not enough: the Welsh Guards returned to England with only around half the men it had left with and the Irish Guards had lost around a third. Lieutenant Colonel Dean of the AMPC was knocked unconscious by the blast of a shell but recovered just in time to become the last senior officer to escape before the town fell. The next day, the *Daily Mirror* headlined its war news 'The Hell that was Boulogne'. Few who had been there would disagree.

French troops arrive at a British port after the evacuation.

JUNKERS JU 87 'STUKA'

Crew: 2
Maximum Speed: 240mph at 13,500ft (390km/h at 4,400m)
Bombs: usually 1 × 250kg bomb under the fuselage and 4 × 50kg bombs under the wings
Guns: 2 × 7.92mm MG 17 machine guns, one facing forward the other operated by a crewman facing the rear
Range: 300 miles (500km)
Ceiling: 27,000ft (8,200m)

Taking its name from the German word *Sturzkampfflugzeug* (dive-bomber), the Junkers Ju 87 was designed to be 'flying artillery', able to dive vertically onto small targets like artillery positions, trenches and headquarters buildings.

Guided onto its target by radio directions from specially trained ground forces, the eerie scream of *Jericho-Trompete* (Jericho trumpet) sirens fitted to the undercarriage meant the Stuka quickly became a powerful propaganda symbol of German air power, spreading terror wherever it appeared. Stuka attacks on refugee convoys added to its fearsome reputation, causing panic and creating gridlock on roads behind the Allied lines, preventing reinforcements from moving forward. But it was off the beaches of Dunkirk that Stukas proved most deadly, attacking Allied ships offshore almost at will.

Stuka bombers set out on a mission. Although later withdrawn from the Battle of Britain, when they proved vulnerable to British fighters, during the battle for France they were highly effective in supporting the ground forces, and especially useful in attacking the evacuation fleet.

AMPC GANG FIGHT

During the fighting for the port of Boulogne, a company of AMPC men recruited from the Glasgow area were ordered by their commander, Lieutenant Colonel Donald Dean, a VC winner in 1918, to try to rescue two outposts surrounded by the Germans. Few of the men had even held a rifle, let alone been trained to use them, but they made their way towards the trapped men. As they made their way through the shattered streets, the company encountered a group of Germans at close range. The AMPC men immediately dropped their rifles and began to run. Hardened Glaswegians do not run away and these men were no exception. Having dropped the rifles they did not know how to use, they charged the Germans with weapons they were familiar with – cutthroat razors they had used many times in gang fights at home. Lieutenant Colonel Dean preferred to use his pistol in the short but bloody battle and was soon able to bring out the men of both outposts safely. He and his men then took over positions guarding access routes to the harbour, allowing troops of the Guards Brigade to evacuate on naval ships. Unlike the Guards officers involved, Dean received no official recognition for his actions at Boulogne.

6

THE BATTLE FOR CALAIS

With Boulogne gone, attention turned to its nearby neighbour, Calais. Back in England, men of the 1st Battalion of Queen Victoria's Rifles, a Territorial motorcycle reconnaissance unit, had handed over their vehicles to reinforce 1st Armoured Division, so it came as something of a surprise to be ordered to prepare to move without a single piece of transport and no training in infantry tactics. Nevertheless, the battalion arrived in Dover, where the sound of the bombardment of Boulogne could clearly be heard, to a confused situation: 3rd Royal Tank Regiment had also been ordered to Calais alongside them but with no instructions about who they were to serve under or where to find orders. The next day, as two battalions of the Rifle Brigade set out from Dover, one man commented, 'the regiment's going the wrong way. if you ask me.' They arrived to find a row of corpses lined up along the quay behind lines of stretcher cases waiting to be taken home.

That night, German forces were making for Dunkirk, leaving 10th Panzer Division to take Calais. What actually happened has never been fully explained, although cracks were appearing in the Anglo-French alliance and many among the French believed that the British had plans to leave their allies behind to cover their own escape. Whatever the truth, on 24 May, French naval gunners stopped firing, spiked their guns and left their positions to make their way to waiting ships for evacuation, whilst at the quayside the French naval commander personally pleaded with departing soldiers and sailors to stay. Addressing around 1,500 men aboard one ship, he found just one volunteer, an artillery officer named Capitaine Michel Blanchardiere. Together the two men eventually rounded up fifty Frenchmen willing to stay.

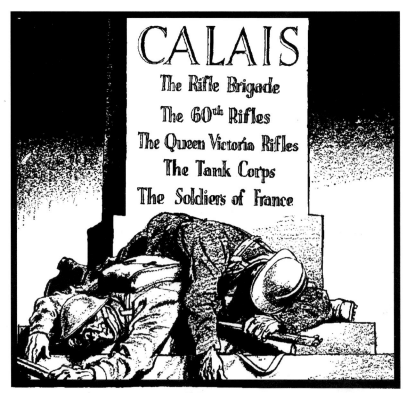

'Their Name Liveth for Evermore!' This illustration appeared in the *Daily Mirror* following the fall of Calais. The accompanying editorial told its readers not to flag because 'to flag would be to prove ourselves pitiably unworthy of those brave men who lie dead along the shores of France'.

Over the next few days, German forces closed in on the Citadel, Calais' main fort, but the British did not give way easily. On 26 May, German commander General Guderian set a deadline: if 10th Panzer Division had not secured Calais by 2 p.m. that day they would be withdrawn and the Luftwaffe would be called in to destroy the town. It was perhaps an overreaction, since that morning a report from Calais to the War Office had described any effort to reinforce them as 'probably a forlorn hope'. That afternoon, the French commander surrendered and British troops, surrounded in the Citadel, had no choice but to follow suit. Isolated groups fought on through the night, but by 27 May the battle was over.

Now only Dunkirk offered any chance of salvation for the BEF.

Navy, Army and Air Force Institute workers Violet Bignell, Gwendoline Stephens and E.J. Davies claimed to be able to adjust their watches by the clock tower in Calais. The sound of the battle could clearly be heard in the English Channel ports.

7

CANAL LINE

As Calais and Boulogne came under attack, the Canal Line also came under pressure. Stretching from La Bassée through Béthune to Gravelines on the coast, it provided the last major barrier to German forces pushing up from the south. Brigadier John Gawthorpe had lost most of his men when 137 Brigade's rail convoy was stopped at Abbeville. He was now tasked with defending a line just north of Béthune from Hinges to St-Omer – a distance of 24 miles – with no fewer than eighteen bridges to hold against attack. With communications between the various headquarters limited to what could be achieved by a few officers on borrowed bicycles, it was immediately clear that the best they would be able to do would be to deny them the bridges and force the Germans to mount a river-crossing operation – a delay of a matter of hours. Gawthorpe's only available infantry, an untrained battalion of the West Yorkshires, had arrived at their destination and been given orders to hold it 'to the last man, the last round'.

All along the canal, scratch forces prepared to do what they could to slow the Germans, at least until better trained and equipped regulars could reinforce them. Every bridge across the canal was crammed with refugees, making it almost impossible to move between positions and check what was happening and, since Gawthorpe had been given just two military policemen on motorcycles to control traffic for the entire area, he decided to use them as messengers instead. By late afternoon on 22 May, every

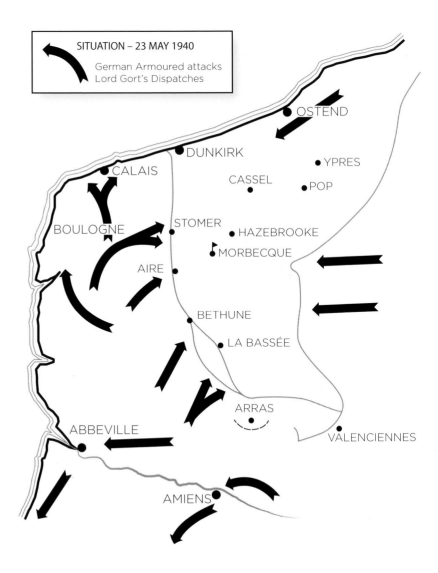

Map of the Canal Line produced by Brigadier Gawthorpe after the battle. (Author's collection)

SITUATION – 23 MAY 1940

German Armoured attacks
Lord Gort's Dispatches

bridge had been prepared for demolition, but the officers responsible for blowing them up worried what they would do if refugees were still crossing when the Germans arrived.

As the various force commanders struggled to fill the gaping voids in their defence lines, the German advance was now swinging northwards. Heading straight towards Hinges were three heavily armed divisions: the Wehrmacht's 3rd Panzer Division and two SS formations – the SS-*Verfügungsdivision* (SS-VT, literally 'Special Reserve Troops') and the SS-*Totenkopf* (Death's Head). Unlike the SS-VT, the *Totenkopf* had not been raised as a military unit but as a police unit to provide concentration camp guards, yet its troops had already earned the distrust of their *Wehrmacht* colleagues for their thuggish behaviour in Poland. Under their fanatical commander, Theodor Eicke, recruits had been required to renounce their religion and swear loyalty only to the Führer. Now, following much political manoeuvring, Eicke had had his unit assigned combat duties after a winter of intensive military training. Held in reserve during the first attacks, the *Totenkopf* were angered by rumours fuelled by Rommel and his men that the SS had panicked in their first encounter with British tanks at Arras. Humiliated, their response had been to murder ninety-two civilians in the town of Aubigny-en-Artois and another forty-five in the villages of Vandélicourt and Berles-Monchel early on 22 May, as they headed towards the Canal Line. They were keen to avenge themselves.

Also moving north that day were the remnants of those units bypassed by the Arras attack. Elements of the British 2nd, 44th and 48th Divisions were all beginning to arrive in the Béthune–La Bassée area. By nightfall, Gawthorpe's command had expanded with the allocation of troops from two Royal Engineer (RE) Chemical Companies, two RE Field Companies, three Belgian anti-tank guns, one company each of Northumberland Fusiliers and the 'Don Detail' battalion, formed from men taken from base camps and transit depots who had not been able to return to their own units. Then, that evening, the first probing attacks began.

Treading more carefully after the Arras counterattack, *Hauptsturmführer* (Captain) Johannes Muhlenkamp's 15th Motorcycle Infantry Company of the SS-VT, equipped with motorcycles and sidecars armed with machine guns, had reached the canal that afternoon. Shortly after midnight, isolated shots rang out along the line of the canal as SS patrols probed forward on either side of Gawthorpe's

German SS troops advancing across the Canal Line. (Author's collection)

men. To the north, *Untersturmführer* (Second Lieutenant) Schulze approached the outskirts of Aire at the head of a small motorised column containing his reinforced platoon of the SS-VT and a few anti-tank guns. He had been tasked with securing the Aire bridge, and in the pitch darkness he took his troops into the town. About halfway along the street, Schulze found his path blocked by a vehicle and realised it was part of a column stretching down the road and creeping forward. Assuming that they were tanks of 3rd Panzer outside their sector, he tagged along behind as they made their way through the town. The stop–start movement of the tanks infuriated him and, impatient to get on with his mission, he climbed aboard the nearest tank and rapped on the turret with his pipe only to be greeted by a torrent of French. Wisely keeping quiet, he dismounted and ordered his men to unhitch the anti-tank guns and move them to the side of the street. They opened fire at point-blank range and, leaving a trail of twenty burning tanks along Aire's main street, Schulze withdrew.

All along the Canal Line, road and rail bridges were blown – one of them even as German engineers attempted to remove the charges – but groups of infantry found ways across and began to approach the defenders. Eicke's men were regaining confidence and he became determined that they would break through the British and redeem themselves at all cost. Despite his orders to simply look for potential crossing points around Béthune, Eicke sent his men across without any reconnaissance, and it was only when his men reached the far side that they discovered how strongly the British were dug in. The Germans were soon forced back, but by evening a second attempt had been made and by nightfall the West Yorkshires were in danger of being surrounded. They were only saved when Hitler himself ordered all German forces to stop their attacks.

Infuriated, Eicke began to pull his men back, only to find British fire intensifying as they recognised the withdrawal. Artillery fire was brought in from north of Béthune and it soon became clear that an orderly operation was out of the question. Abandoning their kit, Eicke's SS troopers were thrown into a headlong race for the canal where they simply jumped in and swam for the safety of the far bank, leaving behind forty-two dead, 121 wounded and five missing. Once

HALT ORDER

On 24 May, German commanders received orders to stop their advance. Panzer leader Heinz Guderian described his staff as 'utterly speechless' when they received the order but was unable to argue against it as no explanation was offered for the decision.

The Halt Order has been the subject of historical debate ever since. Claims that Hitler wanted to let the British off lightly in the hopes of a negotiated peace have been suggested, but a directive issued that day, demanding the annihilation of all Allied forces in the Dunkirk pocket and ordering the Luftwaffe to prevent their escape, proves that was not the reason. Other theories include: a pause to prevent the German tanks running out of fuel as they outran their supply lines; time for the infantry to catch up with the fast-moving Panzer forces; a recognition that the countryside around Dunkirk was filled with waterways that would make it difficult to use tanks there; a need to conserve tanks for use in *Fall Rot* (Plan Red, code name for the conquest of the rest of France); or that the Luftwaffe commander Hermann Göring had used his influence to persuade Hitler to allow the air force to destroy the Allied armies on the beaches. Whatever the rationale, it is clear that both the British and German commanders agreed that the fate of the Allied army was sealed.

Leading Army Group A's advance through Belgium, General Gerd von Rundstedt later called the Halt Order 'one of the great turning points of the war'. The order lasted until 26 May, allowing crucial time for the Royal Navy to put Operation Dynamo into action and consequently save the BEF.

back across, Eicke found his corps commander waiting for him, having witnessed the debacle. His already low opinion of the SS had been confirmed by what he had seen and he is alleged to have called Eicke a 'butcher' to his face. For two days, a furious Eicke and his men sat in pouring rain south of the Canal Line waiting for the order to be lifted, as British mortar and artillery fire kept up a steady bombardment.

The British, meanwhile, were using the pause to replace the West Yorkshires with regular troops. Around Hinges, the 2nd Royal Norfolks began taking over on the night of the 24–25th, and by the 27th the West Yorkshires had moved into a rest area a few miles away. By then the *Totenkopf* had finally resumed their attack, and had now been given the task of securing the area around Hinges and pushing north. Against a defence so desperate that when British troops ran out of ammunition they fought on with bayonets and entrenching tools, the military ineptitude of Eicke and his officers led to men being ordered to attempt frontal assaults on machine-gun positions in the belief that brute force and ignorance could achieve as much as skill and training. When the 2nd Norfolks finally surrendered, the SS were once again embarrassed by their own incompetence and eager to take their frustration out on their prisoners; all the unarmed prisoners were murdered in cold blood. Including the victims of this atrocity, Eicke had inflicted around 300 casualties on the British, but his poor leadership of the *Totenkopf* had cost twice that many casualties among his own men – some 155 dead, 483 wounded and fifty-three missing.

As his men marched away from the Canal Line, Brigadier Gawthorpe received orders to head for the town of Cassel perched atop one of the very few hills in Flanders and an ideal defensive position. It fell to a German assault before he could reach it. Instead, a staff officer in the village of Steenvoorde told him 'to take no further aggressive action [and] report to III Corps headquarters at Teteghem, near Dunkirk, with all you've got'. When Gawthorpe protested that Dunkirk was on the English Channel, the reply was short and to the point: 'We happen to be going that way.'

Far left: Blowing a bridge to delay the enemy. Sometimes refugees were still crossing. (Author's collection)

Left: German infantry and tanks during the fighting on La Bassée Canal. (Author's collection)

8

STUBBORN RESISTANCE

On 20 May a meeting of senior naval officers was held at Dover Castle, under the command of Vice Admiral Bertram Ramsay, to discuss plans to evacuate the BEF from France should it become necessary.

In most places the Channel is so shallow that if St Paul's Cathedral could be placed in it, the dome would break the surface – between Dover and Calais the average depth is just 45m. Shallow water meant large vessels could not pick men up from the beaches without running aground, and even if they could they would be vulnerable to artillery fire and bombing. A further complication was the fact that

Allied forces in Norway were also being evacuated, adding to the pressure on the navy's resources, which were by now stretched to the limit. The only option would be to use civilian vessels.

Fortunately, a week earlier the BBC had broadcast an order from the Admiralty 'requesting all owners of self-propelled pleasure craft between 30 and 100 feet in length to send all particulars to the Admiralty within fourteen days from today if they have not already been offered or requisitioned'. The original intention was to use these private boats as naval auxiliaries for harbour patrols and coastal duties, but as a result of this order the navy had at its disposal a fleet ranging from luxury yachts to pre-war ferries, paddle steamers and even a flotilla of forty motorised Dutch coastal barges handed over just before the Dutch surrender. If the ports of Calais, Boulogne and Dunkirk remained in Allied hands, naval planners estimated that up to 3,000 men per day could be evacuated. It would mean the loss of the majority of the BEF, but at least the nucleus of a new army could be saved. Since the meeting was held in a room formerly used to house an electrical plant known as the 'dynamo room' the operation would be named Operation Dynamo. As naval planners struggled with the logistics of ensuring that sea lanes were swept for mines and cover was available to guard against U-boat attacks, the task became ever harder, as first Calais and then Boulogne fell. The likelihood of saving even 3,000 men a day became more and more remote.

On 14 May, the Royal Navy began gathering boats over 30ft in length for a variety of tasks. Many would sail to Dunkirk with naval crews, others would arrive with their owners once the evacuation got under way.

The flotilla of 'little ships' being towed back up the River Thames after helping to save
the lives of thousands of Allied troops from Dunkirk.

On 25 May, a British patrol under Sergeant Burford of the Middlesex Regiment crossed the River Lys in a small boat and encountered German troops. As the two sides fought, a German staff car drove into Burford's path; Burford opened fire, killing the driver. The passenger escaped, leaving behind a briefcase, which turned out to contain top-secret German plans for a campaign that Burford managed to take back to headquarters. Although worried it may be a deliberate trick, Gort examined the plans and realised that the Germans intended to attack through a gap left by retreating Belgian forces in the area around Ypres.

Under pressure from the French to support another planned counterattack to the south, Gort had only two divisions in reserve and needed to make a decision: either to go ahead with France's plan or to believe the documents and send his troops north to reinforce the Ypres sector. Brussels had already fallen to the Germans and it was only a matter of time before the Belgian Army broke. If he did not reinforce the north, the Germans would almost certainly break through and trap the Allied armies. If, on the other hand, he reinforced the north at the cost of sending men to support the French, he would be open to the inevitable accusations that he had undermined the last chance to snatch victory from the jaws of defeat.

Even as Gort struggled between loyalty to his allies and his duty to protect the BEF, discussions in the Defence Ministry in Paris had already turned to surrender. Early that evening, a report reached Gort that the planned French counterattack scheduled for the next day would now consist of a single division. It was the sign he needed that he should not waste his men on a scheme that in all probability would not take place. He sent his reserves north.

That evening, a meeting in London called for the evacuation of all stores in base areas, or 'at least a proportion of them'. The next morning, the War Cabinet confirmed that indications were that the French would not be able to launch their proposed attack, in which case 'the safety of the BEF will be [the] predominant consideration'. Gort was told, 'fight your way back to west where all beaches and ports east of Gravelines will be used for embarkation. Navy will provide fleet of ships and small boats and RAF [will] give full support. As withdrawal may have to begin very early preliminary plans should be urgently prepared.' However, 'it is obvious you should not discuss the possibility of the move with the French or the Belgians'. In reply, Gort informed the War Cabinet that whatever happened, 'a great part of the BEF and its equipment will be lost'.

The decision was not an easy one. In 1914, when the German Army swept through Belgium and seemed on the verge of destroying the earlier BEF, a similar evacuation had been considered and French generals were quick to talk about the British 'running for the ports' when things got difficult, and angry French politicians and generals spoke of Britain's intention to 'defend itself to the last Frenchman'. Fortunately, British intentions for now coincided with a French plan to withdraw to a perimeter around Dunkirk to create a redoubt 'with no thought of retreat' from which to fight back, so the British move towards the coast did not raise suspicion from their allies. The plan to hold out had some merit; the move could be reinforced by sea and the many canals in the area made it difficult tank country and thus a very defensible position – so much so that when the situation was reversed four years later, Canadian troops did not attempt to take the town by a ground attack and instead laid siege as the rest of the Allied armies pushed on. Dunkirk's German defenders did not surrender until 9 May 1945, the day after Berlin fell.

The perimeter around Dunkirk was divided into three sectors to be defended by British, French and Belgian forces, as thousands of men began to arrive either with their units or as stragglers – none knowing that BEF headquarters expected that even in the best case scenario only around 45,000 of them could possibly be saved. The BEF, by now on half rations and with dwindling stocks of ammunition, began to head west, leaving behind pockets of resistance to act as a

Far left: Some of the private boats, used to assist with the evacuation of over 300,000 Allied troops from Dunkirk, being towed back up the River Thames on their return to England.

Above left: An old paddle steamer, once used as a pleasure boat, typical of the types of ship pressed into service for the evacuation of the BEF from the beaches at Dunkirk.

Bottom left: Winston Churchill (left) and Admiral Bertram Ramsay (centre) in conversation on a return trip to France soon after D-Day, 1944. Ramsay was responsible for the planning and execution of Operation Dynamo.

rearguard. Near Cassel, Major Bill Percy-Hardman and his thirty-one men of the Gloucestershire Regiment faced overwhelming odds but managed to delay the Germans for a day. Nearby, soldiers from a regiment under the command of Second Lieutenant Roy Creswell barricaded themselves into a concrete blockhouse and held out for two full days before finally being forced to surrender. As the men emerged into daylight and captivity, a column of smoke could be seen in the distance. The Germans told them it had acted as marker for where the BEF were evacuating.

Stubborn resistance continued but at a heavy price. The Royal Warwickshire Regiment arrived at the small town of Wormhout early on 26 May to find it quiet. It was only the next day that the first signs of enemy activity began, with a short air raid that alerted the men that an attack was imminent. A German convoy appeared and soon a fierce firefight developed. As the battle raged, *Obergruppenführer* 'Sepp' Dietrich, of the SS *Leibstandarte* Adolf Hitler Regiment, was travelling in his car when it came under fire, killing the driver. Dietrich and another officer were forced to dive into a ditch and were kept pinned down for about four hours, depriving his regiment of its commander and leaving him covered in mud and deeply embarrassed once tanks had to be brought up to rescue him.

The British continued to fire until all 240 rounds of anti-tank ammunition had been used up, leaving the survivors helpless to prevent the German tanks overrunning their positions. Exactly what happened next is unclear. Dietrich was known to have issued orders that no prisoners should be taken and around eighty to ninety men were rounded up and forced into a barn. From there, in batches of five, some were taken out and shot in the back. After three groups had been murdered this way, the Germans entered the barn throwing hand grenades into the crowd of prisoners and machine-gunning them. Of the three companies of 2nd Royal Warwicks who stood their ground, only seven officers and 130 men returned to England.

As desperate rearguard actions held the German advance, troops poured back towards Dunkirk. 'It was now learned,' wrote Lieutenant Jeremy Moor:

that German mechanised forces were closing in on all sides. The men's feet were by this time in poor shape and after Watou, Haringhe and Rousbrugge had been passed, with anti-tank

June 1940. Official advice began to be circulated about what to do in case of invasion. With so many anti-tank weapons lost in France, it was suggested that troops could use steel pipes and girders to jam the tracks of enemy tanks to disable them, killing the crew as they emerged to untangle the wheels. (Author's collection)

JUST TWO OF THE MANY THINGS WE SHOULD ALL BE LEARNING NOW

Right Way to Bar Door . . .
A stout bar placed so under the lock or bolt will keep the strongest man from forcing it.

. . . And the Wrong
All the shock comes across the wood instead of along it. Heavy blows will break the bar across.

Right Way to Shield Window . . . and the Wrong
"Have a piece of canvas or a blanket to put behind the window to catch flying glass. Stretch it on a wooden frame."

"If the cover is placed directly against the window the blast from a hand-grenade can drive straight through it "

weapons in position at the road side all the way, it began to appear doubtful whether the battalion would win its race down the narrowing corridor to the sea.

Moor's battalion war diary noted that by 29 May 'whereabouts of the bulk of the battalion unknown having been scattered on march'. The night before, Lieutenant Clough and Company Sergeant Major Clayton settled down for the night at a farm. They woke the next morning to find they had been left behind by their unit. It was the same everywhere. During the Phoney War there had been little effort to train for route marches and many of the recent arrivals had not even had chance to break their boots in. Men fell behind and were left to fend for themselves; others found transport and made their own way towards the column of smoke that signposted rescue. Survivors reported men who reached the beaches and took off their boots only to find them filled with blood where blisters had been rubbed raw. The only thought for many was to get away – but how?

How to Protect a Car
If you'll have to use a car on the roads, get a mattress ready now to fix on the roof. It and the roof will stop a bullet.

9

'I DO LIKE TO BE BESIDE THE SEASIDE'

On 20 May the French naval commander in charge of Dunkirk, Admiral Abrial, had ordered all merchant ships out of the port to prevent it becoming blocked by sunken ships as the town came under heavy air attack. Even so, by 26 May Dunkirk had seen just under 28,000 men transported back to England, mostly the 'useless mouths' ordered out as soon as the BEF had become trapped, as well as wounded men brought out of the fighting. On the 27th, priorities changed. Now the men lining up for a place aboard the *Mona's Isle* were no longer support troops but front-line infantrymen. The BEF were being ordered out of France and Operation Dynamo was under way.

Mona's Isle left harbour with 1,420 men aboard on that Monday morning, under fire from shore guns as she headed directly for home by the fastest route. Then Messerschmidt fighters pounced, machine-gunning her decks. She arrived in Dover with twenty-three of her passengers dead and sixty wounded. It was a grim taste of what lay ahead. Five other transports had to turn back empty because of the fire from shore batteries. That evening, Captain Bill Tennant arrived to act as Ramsay's representative in Dunkirk and set about examining his options. Finding the place in flames he signalled back that all craft should be directed to the beaches east of the town as soon as possible.

The beaches, with three holiday resorts available to act as assembly areas, were ideal places to gather the men together, but the 20 miles of gently sloping sand and shallow waters were the worst possible place to try to get the men aboard ships. There were no jetties or piers and the only way to get men out to deeper waters where larger ships could safely sail was by using lifeboats to ferry them out. Two naval boats spent the entire night ferrying just 200 men out to a waiting destroyer. Even so, the first day of the evacuation saw over 3,000 British soldiers and 1,250 wounded men taken to Britain, along with around 4,000 French specialists given permission to leave by Admiral Abrial.

Mona's Isle. (Author's collection)

Realisation that British fighting troops were boarding ships for home came as a shock to the French, although it was recognised by many that, given the overall situation, there was no real alternative. Nevertheless, tensions rose as 'perfidious Albion' seemed set on abandoning its allies. A ship set aside for French troops was boarded by British soldiers who, angered when they found the ship was destined for Cherbourg to deliver the Frenchmen back into the fighting south of the Somme, began throwing weapons overboard in the belief that this would force the French to go to Britain to rearm. Frenchmen were turned away at gunpoint from British ships and on the beaches there were incidents that almost led to gunfights between Allied contingents. The town of Dunkirk was rapidly filling up with refugees, stragglers, deserters, untrained AMPC men who had endured horrific bombing for days and a whole range of armed

Bravery, Endurance, Fortitude!

"This way, chum!"

Above: 'Bravery, Endurance, Fortitude!' This cartoon appeared in the *Daily Mirror* on 31 May 1940, drawn by its political cartoonist Philip Zec.

Left: 'This way, chum!' *Daily Mirror* cartoon published on 1 June 1940 following the evacuation of British and French troops from Dunkirk.

Left: Armed naval trawler involved in evacuating BEF HQ staff from Dunkirk.

Below left: After a long retreat the bulk of the BEF reached the Dunkirk bridgehead. On 26 May Operation Dynamo – the evacuation – began. The RAF, bitterly maligned at the time by the army, fought vehemently to deny the enemy the total air supremacy that would have destroyed the BEF. It was hoped that some 45,000 men could be evacuated. In total, 338,000 Allied troops were saved, 26,000 of whom were French. On 4 June, Churchill reported to the House of Commons, seeking to check the mood of national euphoria and relief at the unexpected deliverance. His speech became known as 'We shall fight them on the beaches', c. 2 June 1940.

Below: Two ships from the flotilla of ships and little boats that helped in the evacuation of British French and Belgium troops.

and unarmed bands roaming the streets looting and drinking; there were too few military policemen available to restore any kind of order. Tennant himself was confronted with a group determined to force their way onto a ship, but he managed to persuade them to wait for orders. Panic was beginning to set in.

But where there was fear there was also humour. Those who could were put to work directing traffic and putting the final Canal Line into a state of defence. Brigadier Gawthorpe himself stood on the beach directing troops in an effort to maintain calm: 'Right, you join your division over there ... yes you're all going together but you can't go without tickets ... Division's got the tickets.' A group of men were heard singing 'I do like to be beside the seaside' as they waited patiently for their turn. Cries of 'all aboard the Skylark!' rang out when boats arrived, and reports tell of disciplined units standing as if on parade as men were counted off to board the nearest craft.

Private Ernest Jones had celebrated his twenty-first birthday just days before and now arrived with a small group of stragglers: 'Amidst the confusion of abandoned vehicles, flooded fields and disappearing officers,' he later wrote, 'we made our way to the coast.' They reached a square in Dunkirk where the officer who

Above: A naval officer on the beach at Dunkirk to organise the evacuation.

Right: BEF troops wading in the water at Dunkirk to meet the rescue boats.

had led them told them to stay where they were and that he would find transport. He did not return and it was only later that Jones discovered he got home five days before his men. As they waited in the square, the group took shelter from incoming artillery in an air-raid shelter. As they waited, another soldier arrived, tripped and his rifle went off, striking Jones' friend Cyril Rigby in the knee. They managed to get him to a passing ambulance convoy and went with him to the quayside where they found row upon row of ambulances, with the wounded waiting patiently to be carried aboard the next ship to brave the run into the harbour. Told to make their way to the beaches, Jones and his friend 'Chuck' Skillbeck found a stores vehicle and changed into clean uniforms before finding their way to a nearby queue where, in groups of fifty at a time, they moved up to safety aboard HMS *Exeter*. Jones was never able to find out what happened to his wounded friend.

Above: Place Jean Bart before the battle where Ernest Jones and his mates waited for their officer to return, not knowing he had already embarked for home. (Author's collection)

Right: Place Jean Bart after the battle. (Author's collection)

LIGHTOLLER

Among the boats requisitioned by the Admiralty to sail to Dunkirk was *Sundowner*, an old naval tender built in 1912 and renovated by its owner, retired naval officer Charles Herbert Lightoller. Along with his son, Roger, and an 18-year-old Sea Scout named Gerald Ashcroft, Lightoller immediately volunteered to sail her across and on 1 June arrived at Dunkirk, having already rescued the crew of a burning motor cruiser on the way, and began taking men aboard. At just 58ft in length, somehow seventy-five men were crammed into the cabin with another fifty-five on deck: a total of 130 men 'packed so tightly they had to be piled on top of each other'. After running the gauntlet of enemy fire, *Sundowner* delivered her passengers to Ramsgate harbour and prepared to go back until orders preventing any boat with a maximum speed under 20 knots were sent out. His passengers may not have known it, but Lightoller was no stranger to danger at sea: he had been in charge of loading lifeboats on the *Titanic* and only survived because an exploding boiler blasted him back to the surface as the ship went under.

Charles Lightoller (right) and his son, Roger, after their return from Dunkirk.

Above: Behaving almost as if it were a Bank Holiday weekend trip to the seaside, men queued patiently for their ride home.

Left: With nowhere to run or take shelter, the lines of men moving down the Mole jetty in Dunkirk Harbour relied on the few remaining anti-aircraft guns available for protection against raids.

Left and below: Weighed down with heavy equipment, men waded out to sea to reach the little ships. Some stood for hours up to their necks in the cold water.

Above: Under attack by Stuka dive-bombers, troops attempt to reach a boat off the beach.

The tide recedes, revealing the left behind and abandoned overcoats on the sands of Dunkirk.

The blazing oil depot at Dunkirk not only guided the little ships across the Channel, but also soldiers cut off from their units in the retreat – and, of course, the German bombers.

Realising that the harbour itself had become far too dangerous to use, Tennant spotted the East Mole, built as a breakwater but offering almost a mile of berthing space. Early on 28 May, six destroyers arrived alongside and began filling up with troops before setting out on the 87-mile easterly route that, although twice as long as the shorter direct run, avoided the worst of the shore batteries and dangerous shallows around Gravelines. That afternoon, the first of Dunkirk's famous 'little ships' appeared off the beaches. Long lines of men snaked into the sea as they waded out to meet the small craft, whilst in the distance destroyers and larger ships could be seen scurrying to and fro against the pall of black smoke from blazing oil depots on the edge of the town. In what must have been a terrifying version of the post office queue, men waited whilst up to their necks in water for boats to keep their promises to return time and again.

Left: Fires raging in Dunkirk – a striking photograph taken from on board a destroyer.

Above: Allied troops returning home after being rescued on the beaches of Dunkirk. To the left and centre of the photograph are some of the craft and coastal forces that assisted in the mission.

Above and right: Weary troops of the BEF on the decks of the P&A Campbell paddle steamer *Glen Gower* as they make their way home.

Left: Troops of the BEF aboard a transport ship headed for England as they take a last look back at the French coast from where they had just escaped.

Right: Soldiers crowded on board a ship returning from Dunkirk. (Author's collection)

Around 5,000 men escaped this way during the day, less than half the number sailing from the Mole with dry feet.

To the dangers posed by shore batteries and bombers, 29 May brought a new menace when in the darkness before dawn torpedoes from a prowling German E-boat hit two evacuee-filled destroyers. Daylight brought intensified Luftwaffe attacks and that afternoon a raid caught eleven British and two French ships alongside the Mole.

Five vessels were totally destroyed and all the others damaged, leaving the Mole unusable but, even so, almost 48,000 men had been taken off.

The RAF, heavily criticised by many among the ground and naval forces for failing to protect them, redoubled its efforts. It was true that very few British aircraft appeared over the evacuation beaches, but their job was to try to intercept the Germans before they reached their targets. Inland, regular air patrols sought to prevent the bombers getting through, whilst on the beaches men quickly realised that bombs falling on soft sand would become buried before exploding and it would take a direct hit to harm anyone who had dug a trench. As a result, many felt confident to return fire whenever an aircraft appeared.

Thursday 30 May brought a respite. Overcast skies and a heavy RAF presence kept the Germans away and the numbers evacuated shot up. At Bray Dunes, vehicles had been driven into the sea at low tide under the direction of the military police and engineers. With planks tied to their roofs, the line of trucks formed what would become known as the 'Provost Jetty' to speed up the loading of small boats. Elsewhere a minesweeper had been deliberately grounded to allow it to be used as a temporary pier. After the devastating air raid the Mole was again back in operation, with a cordon of troops with fixed bayonets standing by to maintain order in the queues of men waiting to board. Even senior officers were put to work. A young naval lieutenant in charge of a Dutch coastal steamer asked if any of the men he had picked up knew how to use a Lewis machine gun. One soldier responded and was ordered to man the weapon mounted on the poop deck. So, with General Brian Horrocks firing at the attacking bombers, the ship sailed away.

As the perimeter shrank, the War Office issued orders that the evacuation was to be completed by the morning of 1 June and that the estimated 60,000 remaining British soldiers should be clear by then. In fact, the estimate was far too low and almost double that number was either already on the beaches or making their way there. It was now only a matter of time before the Germans broke through the Dunkirk perimeter, and the question was one of how many men and guns could be rescued before time ran out.

There was also the delicate matter of who would be asked to hold the perimeter long enough to allow others to escape. The Belgians had surrendered on 28 May, leaving only the British and French to hold back the German advance. Gort, after being ordered back to Britain by the War Office, visited Admiral Abrial and explained the intention to evacuate British and French troops on an equal basis, even offering Abrial use of the East Mole to get his men out. Given that as the commander of the port the East Mole was under Abrial's command anyway, he was perhaps less impressed by British

generosity than Gort had hoped, but the two men parted amicably with an offer that French General Blanchard, whose command was reduced to a few scattered units, should accompany Gort to safety. Blanchard thanked him but refused.

The day of 31 May saw heavy fighting around the perimeter. It was also the day on which the largest number of men were lifted, despite the fact that the men who had organised the collection points and guided men to departure points had themselves now gone, leaving the battered survivors of the rearguards to find their own way to the improvised jetties or to head towards the columns of smoke over Dunkirk itself. Saturday 1 June, the last day of the planned operation, began with a heavy air raid that left two destroyers (including the Calais veteran HMS *Keith*) sunk and three other ships damaged.

On shore, Major Colvin of the Grenadier Guards had led his men back from their stand at Furnes and was looking for a way to escape. It would prove to be a nightmare journey. After an hour standing up to his neck in the water he set off down the beach, passing wounded men who had been hit by gunfire as German planes strafed the beach. Many would drown when the tide turned but there was little that could be done to save them. He watched in horror as the destroyer he had hoped to be picked up by was hit by Stukas and sunk. After hours in a drifting boat he and fourteen men were thrown into the sea when a bomb struck nearby, and men drowned as cramp set in. Eventually picked up by a passing Thames lighter, Colvin found himself heading back to shore, the skipper determined to pick up some wounded men. A tense overnight journey with men

Right: BEF troops arrive into a British port after their evacuation from Dunkirk.

STATISTICS OF EVACUATION

Date	From the beaches	From Dunkirk Harbour	Total
27 May		7,669	7,669
28 May	5,390	11,874	17,804
29 May	13,752	33,558	47,310
30 May	29,512	24,311	58,823
31 May	22,942	45,072	68,014
1 June	17,348	47,081	64,429
2 June	6,695	19,561	26,256
3 June	1,870	24,876	26,746
4 June	622	25,553	26,175
Totals	**98,671**	**239,555**	**338,226**

Source: Julian Thompson, *Dunkirk: Retreat to Victory*, 2008.

Left: A wounded soldier seen here after being evacuated from Dunkirk.

Right: Soldiers firing back as Stukas attack ships offshore.

Far right: German soldiers relax after the battle. (Author's collection)

on the lookout for E-boats brought the tightly packed lighter safely into Dover early the next morning.

By then, German troops were beginning to reach the beaches and one Belgian report described British troops still firing despite being chest-deep in the sea. Thirty-one ships were sunk that day and a decision had to be made about whether the cost to the navy outweighed the army's needs. Two hospital ships, both clearly marked, were hit as they tried to reach the harbour and an order went out that no more wounded men would be evacuated because the space a stretcher took up could be used by three or four standing men. One officer and ten orderlies of the Royal Army Medical Corps would be left behind with every 100 casualties. As ballots were drawn, wounded men quietly tried to sneak away from the casualty stations, knowing they could not hope to get home but reducing the numbers of casualties and therefore the number of orderlies who would have to remain.

At 11.30 p.m. on Sunday 2 June, after another day of heavy attack, Captain Tennant signalled London: 'BEF evacuated.' Then he, General Alexander and Brigadier Parminter (who had stayed on to act as

embarkation officer at the Mole) boarded a motor launch and sailed up the beaches to look for any British soldiers left behind. Finding none, they turned for home.

Behind them, French troops fought on. Thousands of men had stayed at their posts to ensure that the evacuation could continue and, when a request was made for another attempt to rescue some of the 25,000 defenders, Ramsay could not refuse. He told his tired naval crews:

> I hoped and believed that last night would see us through, but the French, who were covering the retirement of the British rearguard, had to repel a strong German attack and so were unable to send their troops to the pier in time to be embarked. We cannot leave our allies in the lurch, and I must call on all officers and men detailed for further evacuation tonight to let the world see that we never let down an ally.

Yet when the ships returned, they found the troops they had expected to find at the Mole had been sent instead to the beaches. It was too risky for the ships to sit and wait and so by the time the soldiers reached the Mole the ships had gone. It was not just poor organisation, German attacks were still pressing in and scratch forces were being sent back into the line to try to buy time. With space for up to 10,000 men, the ships returned almost empty.

At a jetty in the harbour, British pier master Commander Troup was overseeing the evacuation. As General Lucas of the French 32nd Division boarded a motor launch he paused and looked towards the nearby pier, crowded with over 1,000 men standing four deep. Troup watched as every man snapped smartly to attention. Lucas and his staff clicked their heels, saluted their men and boarded the boat.

At 9 a.m. the next day, Dunkirk's defenders surrendered.

10

EVERY MAN FOR HIMSELF

On 4 June, German troops stood on the beaches of the Channel coast, but the battle was not yet over. The breakthrough of 20 May had cut the British supply lines but not destroyed them. South of the Somme were many thousands of British troops from the Lines of Communication system, working at bases throughout Normandy, Brittany and even as far afield as Marseilles. Also cut off were the 51st Highland Division, who had been stationed on the Maginot Line when the invasion began, and the remnants of the British 1st Armoured Division, not to mention the rest of the French Army. They would now need to be defeated before the Germans could claim to have conquered France.

Rex Flowers, the young clerk who had trudged back from Abbeville with his battalion when their rail convoy had been stopped by the attack of 20 May, was now part of Beauman Division, an improvised formation put together from the untrained Territorials sent to work on the docks at St-Nazaire and Cherbourg, old soldiers serving with the AMPC and men who had been in transit camps on their way home on leave or returning from England when the war started. Brought together and issued weapons from the huge stores depots built to supply the BEF, the Beauman Division joined forces with the French and fought on.

French troops rescued from Dunkirk had been sent almost directly from Dover to Southampton and placed on ships to Cherbourg so they could rejoin the fighting. Canadians and Scots troops of the Lowland Division began arriving in Normandy to help bolster French

plans to hold out as long as possible, but it was a forlorn hope. In a fighting retreat through Normandy and across battlefields that would become famous four years later, the Beauman Division did what it could but it was soon overwhelmed near Rouen. Not far away, the 51st Highland Division made their stand alongside their French allies around the small port of St-Valéry-en-Caux. Few escaped.

After the last ships left Dunkirk, command and control broke down almost entirely. French politicians were arguing for surrender even as their generals ordered suicidal last stands that saw French units fight in vain to try to slow the German onslaught. Soon, the Allies were in retreat again, heading for a planed 'Breton redoubt' to be created on the Atlantic coast, but it soon became clear that this was not realistic. British units instead began to head for the ports of St-Malo, Cherbourg, Brest and St-Nazaire in an attempt to evacuate the men and, more importantly, if Britain was to be able to defend itself, the huge stockpiles of guns, stores and equipment that had been brought to France to supply a long war. The Lines of Communication network supplying the front had stretched across France, and as well as the British and the Canadians who had just arrived, there were Indian troops, men from across France's empire, Poles and Czechs who had fled their own countries to continue the fight and even British expats who had set up home in France and who had now arrived at the ports with their French families in tow. As the BEF regrouped in England, naval crews were again pressed into service to repeat the ordeal of Dunkirk.

French troops at a British port before being sent back across the Channel to rejoin the battle in Normandy.

OPERATION AERIAL

Evacuated from French ports 15–25 June 1940

British 144,171

Polish 24,352

French 18,246

Czech 4,938

Belgian 163

Civilians 30–40,000

Source: Major L.F. Ellis, *The War in France and Flanders*, 1953

Postcard of RMS *Lancastria*. Her sinking would lead to the greatest loss of life in British maritime history but the story was immediately suppressed and quickly forgotten. (Author's collection)

On the day France formally surrendered, the Cunard liner RMS *Lancastria*, fresh from its role in the evacuation of Norway, arrived at St-Nazaire as part of a fleet sent with orders to 'load as many men as possible without regard to the limits set down under international law'. With a capacity of 1,700 passengers and 375 crew, Captain Rudolph Sharp and his men began boarding soldiers, RAF personnel, employees of the Belgian branch of Fairey Aviation and civilian refugees as quickly as possible. At 1.50 p.m., the nearby *Oronsay* was hit by a German bombing raid and Captain Sharp was advised to leave, but he delayed because sailing without a destroyer escort would put his ship at risk of submarine attack. *Oronsay* remained in the sea lanes about 10 miles from St-Nazaire itself.

Two hours later a new air attack began and three direct hits caused the *Lancastria* to list and then roll over, sinking within twenty minutes. The order 'Every man for himself' was given as the ship went down and men jumped from the decks. Sapper Cyril Cumbes recalled seeing four men whose necks had been broken by the lifebelts they wore riding up as they hit the water. Other men clambered down the sloping side of the ship as it began to roll and were haunted by the faces of trapped men at the portholes. For Ken Belsham of the Royal Army Pay Corps, the abiding memory would be the guilt he carried after having to dive under the water to avoid the clutches of drowning men. Walter Hirst of the Royal Engineers later remembered:

> There was panic and chaos. Two soldiers at either end of the ship began to open up with Bren guns on the attacking enemy aircraft. After entering the water a seemingly crazed man tried to remove my lifejacket, but I managed to fight him off. I was in the water for around two hours before being picked up. At one point a large Labrador dog swam past which I later discovered belonged to some Belgian refugee children who did not survive the sinking.

In the rush to evacuate no records had been kept and no one knew how many had been aboard although reports state that a soldier heard Captain Sharp and Chief Officer Harry Grattidge discussing the situation and saying that there were 6,700 people aboard and that the next batch would be the last. Estimates of the number of people on the ship as it prepared to sail vary from 4,000 to 9,000, and the

LOSS OF THE 'LANCASTRIA'

The Cunard liner ' Lancastria ' (16,243 tons) was sunk by a
formation of Junkers 87 dive-bombers off St.Nazaire on June 17,
1940. There were about 5,000 British troops on board, and
more than 2,000 of them were lost. Our photographs show :
above, the ' Lancastria ' in her cruise-liner days ; left, settling
down after the enemy attack ; below, heeling over, her pro-
pellers above water ; bottom, troops clustered on the hull and
in the water. Many were rescued by the Royal Navy.
Photos, Associated Press

death toll is equally vague. The official figure of known deaths is 1,738 but claims range as high as 5,800. It is widely accepted that the toll exceeds the combined losses of both the *Titanic* and the *Lusitania*, making the loss of the *Lancastria* the worst in British maritime history. Fearing the impact on public morale, news of the sinking was immediately suppressed.

For weeks after the surrender of France groups of men continued to make their escape from France through ports along the western seaboard or by travelling down to the Mediterranean. Efforts to assist carried on until 14 August, by which time some 191,870 men had been evacuated; between 19 and 23 June, 22,656 civilians left the Channel Islands for sanctuary in England. Hundreds of guns, thousands of vehicles including tanks and many thousands of tons of fuel, ammunition and stores were brought back by the courage and professionalism of naval and civilian crews in an operation now almost forgotten. They would be used to rebuild the shattered army and pave the way for the return to French shores just four years later.

Left: French troops write letters home at a British port before being sent back across the Channel.

Above: Although it was widely believed, even today, that news of the sinking of the *Lancastria* was covered up, in fact Churchill only placed a temporary order suppressing the news because he felt that if it came on the day of the French surrender, the impact on civilian morale would be severe. These pictures were released to the press later that month and the scale of the losses clearly reported. (Author's collection)

Right: Wounded soldiers aboard a train in southern England.

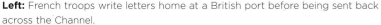

Above: The arrival of French troops in a British port on the south coast.

Right: Crammed aboard a naval ship, British troops arrive back in England. Packed tightly on the decks, they were easy targets for enemy air attack.

The aftermath of the battle on the sands of Dunkirk.

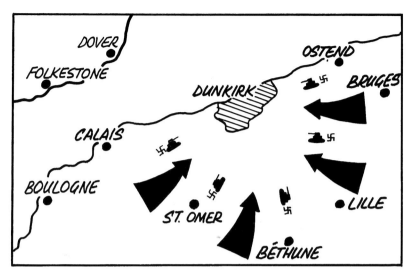

Top left: A map of the German advance and the evacuation of the BEF from the beaches at Dunkirk, June 1940.

Top right: Dunkirk Harbour before the war. (Author's collection)

Above: Place Jean Bart, Dunkirk, after the battle. (Author's collection)

Right: Abandoned equipment on Dunkirk beach front. (Author's collection)

Above left: Abandoned equipment on the streets of Dunkirk. (Author's collection)

Above: Smoke from burning oil depots acted as a marker for troops and ships making their way to Dunkirk. (Author's collection)

Left: Air raid on Dunkirk. (Author's collection)

Right: Some of those left behind.
(Author's collection)

Below right: Exhausted troops sleeping at a makeshift army camp in southern England after their return from France. Across the Channel, a new battle was just about to start.

Below: A German propaganda photograph of a British 'survivor'.
(Author's collection)

Above left: Tired troops sleep in a camp after their return to England.

Above: Operation Ariel: with the BEF shattered, it was vital to get back as many men and as much equipment as possible before the Germans could reach the main British supply depots. (Author's collection)

Left: Troops of the Border Regiment, part of the improvised Beauman Division named after the commander of the supply lines, make their way towards Cherbourg.

Men of the Beauman Division during the retreat through Normandy. (Author's collection)

St-Valéry-en-Caux before the war. Trapped alongside their French allies, the men of the 51st Highland Division made their stand around the town. (Author's collection)

Abandoned vehicles on the road to Cherbourg, Normandy. (Author's collection)

Above: Map of the battle of St-Valéry. (Author's collection)

Left: German soldiers with French colonial troops. The French army included men from its overseas territories in North and West Africa and Southeast Asia. A number of these soldiers were murdered after their surrender and the future for these men in Nazi captivity would be bleak. (Author's collection)

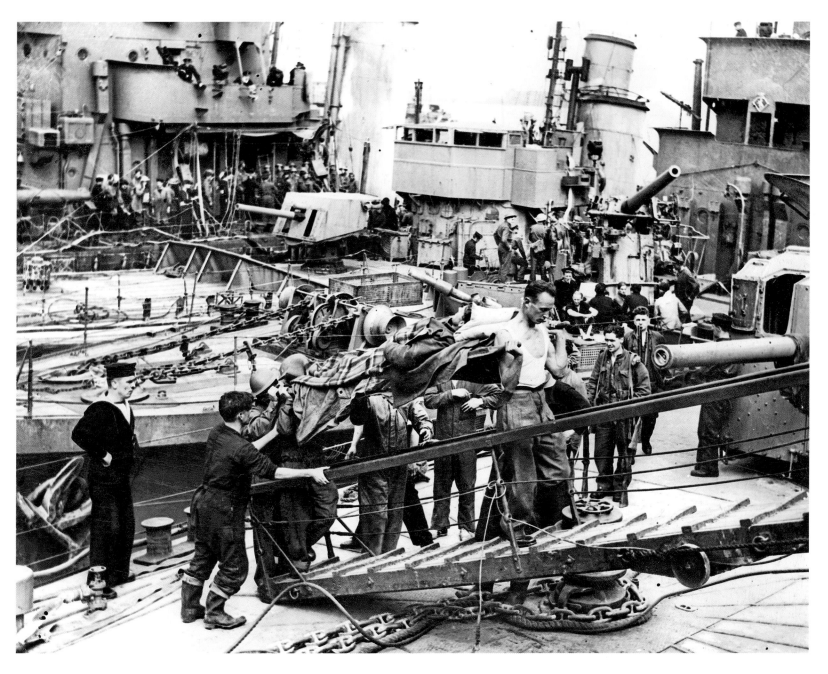

Wounded soldiers carried ashore from the transport ship on arrival in England.

Left: BEF soldiers, injured during the retreat, make their way from the docks to one of the waiting trains.

Right: BEF troops aboard a destroyer as they arrive home from France.

'THIS WAS THEIR FINEST HOUR'

What General Weygand has called the Battle of France is over ... the Battle of Britain is about to begin. Upon this battle depends the survival of Christian civilisation. Upon it depends our own British life, and the long continuity of our institutions and our Empire. The whole fury and might of the enemy must very soon be turned on us. Hitler knows that he will have to break us in this island or lose the war. If we can stand up to him, all Europe may be freed and the life of the world may move forward into broad, sunlit uplands. But if we fail, then the whole world, including the United States, including all that we have known and cared for, will sink into the abyss of a new dark age made more sinister, and perhaps more protracted, by the lights of perverted science. Let us therefore brace ourselves to our duties, and so bear ourselves, that if the British Empire and its Commonwealth last for a thousand years, men will still say, 'This was their finest hour.'

Winston Churchill, 18 June 1940

11

A HERO'S WELCOME

One day in late May 1940, 8-year-old Pauline Spackman was swinging on the front gate of her family home. She did not want to be inside where her 13-year-old sister's coffin had been placed in the front room awaiting the funeral the next day and where her mother, already ill, was quietly grieving. Her soldier father, Clifford, was with the BEF but there was no news of him. As Pauline swung to and fro, she saw a man walking towards her looking 'old scruffy and very tired'. It was only then that she recognised him. 'As I went to sleep that night I felt very sad,' she later wrote, 'as I could hear them both sobbing quietly. I grew up that night and knew I would never be the same again.'

Across the country, exhausted men made their way home. Don Clark arrived in Plymouth on the last day of Operation Ariel to find thousands of women lining the streets outside the harbour asking 'if we had seen their husbands, sons and boy-friends while on our way to the coast in France. They held out photographs of their missing loved ones and pleaded with us for news ... It was a harrowing, unbelievably sad and grief stricken struggle for us to get through them and up to the station.'

Behind them, thousands of men marched into five long years of captivity, among them Jim Laidler, the young recruit who had faced the tanks at Fichieux, near Arras. Others would find ways home over the coming months. Lance Corporal John Warner of the Queen's Regiment slipped away from his captors and, on a bike given to him by a French family, cycled to neutral Spain and reached home in time for his twenty-first birthday. Lance Corporal Downing and Private Ash of the Yorkshire Light Infantry made it into the unoccupied zone of France but were detained by the French and handed over to the Germans when the Vichy government was taken over in 1942. Their comrade Private Winslade was more successful. Without a map, money or any ability to speak either language, he travelled through France and into Spain, making it to Gibraltar and then home. In the West Yorkshire mess, Captain Wilkins, last seen outside Robecq in May 1940, was treated to a hero's welcome when he reached home on 14 August 1941 after over a year on the run.

Alone or in groups, the BEF came home. After a brief period of leave they returned to their units and prepared for what would come next. Bloodied but unbowed, they made ready to go back to France.

BEF survivors in Bristol, 1 July 1940.

Above: BEF troops on the *Skylark* transport ship, 3 June 1940.

Above right: BEF troops return from Dunkirk, June 1940.

Right: A survivor reaches home.

Above: Wounded BEF troops arrive at a Midland hospital after the evacuation of Dunkirk.

Above right: With his ordeal in Dunkirk behind him this soldier takes a well-earned break from the action to read his paper.

Right: Dogs, cats, rabbits and even parrots abandoned by their owners were rescued by British soldiers during the retreat and joined the evacuation.

Above: The *Daily Mirror* reports on the evacuation, 5 June 1940.

Above right: A BEF soldier returning from Flanders in Belgium sends a postcard home from a railway station in the south of England, June 1940.

Right: Volunteers supply refreshments to the troops arriving home from Dunkirk.

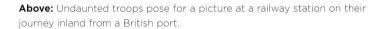

Above: Undaunted troops pose for a picture at a railway station on their journey inland from a British port.

Above right: A welcome drink for jubilant troops as the train pulls up at a railway station following the evacuation.

Right: French soldiers give the thumbs-up as they travel inland from a British port after evacuation.

A group of soldiers chatting to women following their evacuation from Dunkirk, c. 1940.

Cornishman Cecil Collins grabs a snack and entertains his mates as they wait for orders at a port in England.

A group of BEF soldiers posing for a photograph shortly after their arrival in Cardiff.

A soldier giving the thumbs-up following evacuation, 2 June 1940.

Missing bits of uniform, a group of BEF veterans cheer a visiting VIP at a camp in Bristol, although one man seems more interested in the camera than the visitors.

Andre van Campenhout (right), head of the Minister's Office at the Belgian Ministry of Communication and Economic Affairs, invests Hector Annijs with the OBE and the Croix de Guerre at a Welsh town for his bravery in bringing refugees and soldiers to safety in England from Dunkirk, 26 August 1941.

Pleasure steamer *Royal Eagle* back in use on the River Thames after being used for the Dunkirk evacuations, *c*. 1948.

BEF survivors in Bristol, 1 July 1940.

BIBLIOGRAPHY

Blaxland, G., *Destination Dunkirk: The Story of Gort's Army* (London: Wm Kimber, 1973)

Ellis, L.F., *The War in France and Flanders, 1939–1940* (London: HMSO, 1953)

Levine, J., *Forgotten Voices of Dunkirk* (London: Ebury Press, 2010)

Lynch, T., *Dunkirk, 1940: Whereabouts Unknown* (Stroud: The History Press, 2010)

Murland, J., *Retreat and Raeguard: Dunkirk 1940* (Barnsley: Pen & Sword, 2016)

Sebag-Montefiore, H., *Dunkirk: Fight to the Last Man* (London: Penguin, 2007)

Shaw, Frank & Joan Shaw, *We Remember Dunkirk* (Oxford: ISIS, 1997)

Thompson, J., *Retreat to Victory* (London: Sidgwick & Jackson, 2008)

The History Press

The destination for history
www.thehistorypress.co.uk